NEITHER YESTERDAYS NOR TOMORROWS

VIGNETTES of a HOLOCAUST CHILDHOOD

by

George J. Elbaum

1/20/17

To Sarah, with thanks
for what you do, now
and will do in the future.
George

Author contact: gelbaum@alum.mit.edu

School speaking events: www.neitheryesterdays.com

I wrote this for my son Jordan

because it's his heritage

***

I dedicate it to my mother Pauline

whose strength and wits saved us

This book owes its very existence to Mimi Jensen, my wife and life's partner. On many occasions over the years she has urged me to write it, and inspirations such as our visit to Yad Vashem or seeing the movie "Paper Clips" are due to her. She helped edit the book, found the family photos we used in it, and her general enthusiasm for it enhanced my efforts. For her invaluable role in this project, as in my life, my heartfelt gratitude.

A warm Thank You also to Rabbi Michelle Fisher, the Executive Director of MIT Hillel, for her encouragement, editorial suggestions, and efforts to teach me Hebrew by email.

CONTENTS

Introduction - San Francisco 2009

I was one year old in Warsaw in September 1939 when Hitler invaded Poland and World War II started. Within weeks my father was called into the army and never returned, so I never knew him. Within two or three years my grandparents, uncles and aunts, almost a dozen family members in all, had been killed by the Nazis. Only my mother and I were still alive. We were Jewish, so according to the Nazi plan, we were alive illegally. My mother dyed her hair blond and bought the ID documents of a Catholic woman who had died. I neither looked nor knew that I was Jewish, so shortly after my 3rd birthday my mother smuggled me out of the Warsaw ghetto, then paid various Polish Catholic families to hide me and raise me with their own children. I never knew when my mother would visit me, nor if she would. On some visits she took me to a new family with whom I would live for a while and sometimes she told me a new last name that I must remember in case anyone asked who I was. This tenuous life went on for almost 4 years till the war ended and I was almost 7, then to a lesser extent for another 4 years which included my being sent to France, where only a broken leg kept me from continuing to Palestine. I returned to Poland, but stability came only when my mother and I arrived in the U.S. in late 1949. Thinking about those years, I realize that most of my past was painful, sometimes too painful to remember, and my future was so uncertain and unpredictable that I did not plan or anticipate things. I learned to live in the present, with neither yesterdays nor tomorrows to enjoy or console myself, and to some extent this habit has remained into my adulthood. I refused to relive the wartime tragedy through books and films, as my mother did, and I avoided making long-term or strategic plans, preferring to tackle each situation as it came. For years my wife and friends suggested that I put my most poignant experiences to paper, if for no one else than for my son, yet I ignored their suggestions. Even a 1995 visit to the Holocaust memorial in Jerusalem did not change my mind, though it made me understand that my mother, who saved me and herself by luck and strength and wits, all with full awareness of the constant danger and death (which I was too young to understand), could not have come through this horrible experience without some deep emotional scarring.

Apparently I was not yet ready to visit my yesterdays. Then a few months ago I saw the film "Paper Clips" about a middle school in a small Tennessee town whose project on diversity was to explore the Holocaust and, as part of it, to collect 6 million paper clips from around the world to symbolize the 6 million victims of the Nazis. One of the film's scenes shows a meeting of the students and teachers with a group of aged Holocaust survivors who travelled from New York to meet with the students and tell their personal stories. These painful stories of the survivors were very familiar to me, but the heartfelt response and tears of the students and teachers who, for the first time, were face to face with the personal side of the Holocaust, moved me beyond any previous encounters and memories. When the film ended and my wife again suggested, as she had many times before, that I document my memories, I thought for a moment, took a deep breath, and said "I will." And the next day I started.

***

August 20, 1941 - Warsaw ghetto

My mother woke me early, told me that it was my 3rd birthday, and that she had something to show me. Still half asleep, I watched her step back from my bed and then I saw it: a red tricycle standing a few feet away! I still remember jumping out of bed, onto the tricycle, and riding in circles around her. That is my earliest memory, certainly my earliest happy memory, since most of those that followed it for the next several years were anything but.

Still on the tricycle in my pajamas, I followed my mother to the front door as she left for work, then asked my grandmother to take me to the park so I could ride it there. She replied that breakfast came before park, so we did our usual morning routine: she would put two eggs on a low table for me to choose one of them for breakfast, I would then spin each one, chose the one that spun faster and didn't wobble (I have no idea why I did that), and she would scramble it for my breakfast. That day she also told me that since it was my 3rd birthday and I was now a big boy, I could eat with a regular spoon, like the ones she and my mother used, rather than a small twisted one that I had been using. (Decades later I saw in a magazine a photo of a spoon with an S-curve twist in the handle, with an explanation that these were used in old Europe to counter left-handed tendencies in children, and suddenly I recalled my small twisted spoon.) Later that day I was proudly riding my new tricycle in a park when a boy asked me to take him for a ride. I still recall how grown-up I felt when I answered very seriously that the *rama* (the frame between the seat and the handlebars, and one of the few Polish words that I still remember) was too short for him to sit on.

On our return from the park I have a vague recollection of the apartment seeming noisy and crowded with strangers. My grandmother told me they were friends and would be living with us because they lost their home. (Much later, after the war, I learned that this was common, as Jews from other parts of Warsaw were forced into the ghetto and had to live wherever they could, be it with friends or relatives or on the street.)

***

Umschlagplatz
(German for "collection or loading point")

Suddenly there was loud shouting coming from the courtyard, then the entire apartment complex was filled with ear-splitting noise: shouts, screams, doors banging everywhere, and heavy running footsteps. My grandmother ran into the room holding my coat, grabbed my hand and led me to the staircase which was filled with people, all going downstairs. When we reached the courtyard it was already full of people, crowded together in groups, with soldiers in dark-green uniforms shouting and walking between the groups. My grandmother held my hand tightly as we were pushed back-and-forth by the crowd till finally we were standing at the edge of our group, facing the large arched entry gate that led from the street into our courtyard. It seemed we stood there a long, long time, and I recall being glad that my grandmother put my coat on me, and seeing some groups being led by soldiers out of the courtyard through the big gate. Then suddenly I saw my mother running in through the gate holding a piece of paper in her hand, showing the paper to some soldiers, talking with them, and finally coming to us and leading us out of the courtyard. It was only years later, after the war, did I understand what happened: the Nazis were emptying out Warsaw ghetto, apartment block at a time, and shipping the residents to concentration camps. My mother, who was working at a factory in the ghetto which the Germans authorized the American Jewish Joint Distribution Committee ("JOINT") to manage and make uniforms for the German army, somehow learned that our apartment block was being emptied that day, and got from the factory director an official document allowing her to keep her family in place. With this document, in effect a temporary permit to continue living, she managed to convince the German officer commanding that day's sweep to let us go. Had she arrived a few minutes later, it might have been too late.

***

The Shed

"We can only speak in whispers here," my grandmother told me. We were now in a large shed, with corrugated metal walls and ceiling, pieces of rusting metal equipment strewn about, and our bags and blankets on the floor. Several families were here with us, though no one that I recognized, all with bags, suitcases, and blankets. One family even had a little black dachshund, and they told us that it never barks. I petted his soft fur. Some of the people played cards, some knitted, but no one talked except in quiet whispers. My grandmother took some bread and sausage from her bag, made tea on a small primus burner, and that was our dinner. When it got dark, no one lit any candles. We wrapped ourselves in our blankets and slept. I woke up in the morning and wanted to pet the little dachshund, but it was gone. I asked its owners where it is, but their only answer was that it's gone. (Years later, my mother told me that during the night its owners had to choke it to keep it from barking at footsteps near the shed.) The day, or perhaps days, went slowly in the near silence, the only sounds coming from outside the shed. There was a big hole in the shed's roof through which I watched white clouds on the blue sky. Once I saw an airplane with black crosses on its wings flying across the sky. At the time I didn't know that it was a German airplane and the black crosses were the German insignia. It looked so beautiful to me against the blue sky, not constrained in a dark shed as I was, and I felt strangely drawn to it, wanted to be in it, wanted to be with it. I've never lost that feeling and an interest in airplanes: a few years later after the war I read avidly the Polish aviation magazine "Wings and Motor", then in high school in Oregon

I built and flew model airplanes, in college I majored in aeronautical engineering, then worked in the aerospace industry, took flying lessons, got a private pilot license, and for 20 years flew hang gliders in California. However, I have never forgotten that airplane against the blue sky through the hole in the roof, and the feeling of awe and exhilaration it gave me.

***

The Bunker and the Uniform Factory

I don't remember when I last saw my grandmother, under what circumstances, or how my mother explained to me her absence. Years later, after the war, my mother told me that she had bought for my grandmother a place in a "bunker", the name used for the secret hiding places that were being constructed surreptitiously in some buildings in the ghetto, usually behind false walls in the basements. These bunkers were, in effect, Noah's arks of hoped-for survival: places in them were sold for a king's ransom, they were stocked with food for months or years, and with their occupants inside they were sealed and the entrance hidden to prevent detection by the Germans.   Thus once my grandmother was in the bunker my mother assumed that she'd arranged for her safety and could then focus on getting herself and me out of the ghetto.   However, there was a fatal flaw in these plans: while all construction on the bunkers was done by Jews living in the ghetto, the necessarily large quantity of food had to be procured and brought from the "Aryan" (i.e. non-Jewish) side of the ghetto's walls, and in this case the food seller betrayed the bunker's location to the Germans, and all its occupants were immediately sent to concentration camps.

With my grandmother no longer there to care for me, my mother took me with her to her workplace, the JOINT-managed factory in the ghetto making uniforms for the German army. Since all who worked there were Jews I was relatively safe, except during periodic inspections by the Germans. While I didn't understand any of this, my mother sometimes told me to get under a table stacked with dark green uniforms, then stack some more uniforms around me and tell me to be absolutely quiet until she came to get me. I can't really judge now how often she hid me among the uniforms, nor how many days I went to the factory with her, but almost 60 years later, in 2002, I saw this very scene again: the bleak uniform factory and the stacks of dark green uniforms, the gray, somber workers, and I suddenly felt a huge lump in my throat. It was a scene in the movie "The Pianist".

***

The Soup and the Machine Gun

It was a cold winter day, and I was sitting at the table eating hot, thick soup. I had been living in this household for some time and my mother would visit me every so often, though as a four-year-old I couldn't really tell how often. There were other people who lived there for a while, then left and someone else took their place. One of the newcomers was a big, blond woman from the city of Lodz whom the others called Lovichanka (meaning "a woman from Lodz"), and I remember not liking her. It was getting dark and someone was lighting a kerosene lamp on the table when there were loud bangs at the front door and shouts in German, then heavy footsteps. For some inexplicable reason, perhaps because I was hungry, I did not get up to see what was happening but continued eating my soup, until I realized that right beside me a German soldier was standing, looking down at me. I looked up, noticed his heavy winter coat and a rifle on his shoulder, but this rifle had a very big barrel with big holes around it (I now know it's the cooling jacket of a machine gun's barrel). I recall staring at it, fascinated by the many holes, then looking at the soldier and smiling, and then continuing to eat my soup. The soldier stood there for a moment more, then moved on, and in a short while he and the others left the house and all was quiet and normal again. Only years later, after the war, did I learn that had I shown any fear the soldier would have made me drop my pants to check if I was circumcised (only Jews were circumcised in Poland), and I would have never reached my 5th birthday.

***

A Beggar with a Burlap Bag

A few days later my mother visited me. As it happened, Lovichanka, the woman from Lodz whom I did not like, was standing beside me when my mother walked into the room, and for some reason I did not move, did not run to my mother, but simply stood there as if frozen. Seeing that, Lovichanka walked up to my mother and spoke to her in a quiet voice. My mother listened, then approached me, took my hand, and led me into another room. I don't recall anything else unusual about her visit that day, or her saying anything to me about Lovichanka (though a few years later, immediately after the war, an unexpected meeting would reignite this conversation). However, late evening a day or two later I was surprised to be awoken by my mother. She dressed me quickly, put on my overcoat, told me to be quiet and led me out to the cold, dark street outside. As we walked, I asked her where we were going, and she replied that she was taking me to another house where nice people lived and that I would live there starting that night. She also said that from now on I should never say that my last name was Sliwowski, as she had taught me some time ago, but from now on my name would be Kochanowski, and I must always remember that.

I think it was the several unexpected things descending so suddenly on me that completely overwhelmed me at that moment: being woken up from deep sleep, the cold dark night, the confusion of changing my last name and being moved once again from an environment I now knew to a yet another strange house with new strangers. I sat down on the snow and started crying uncontrollably. My mother tried to calm me and comfort me, but to no avail – I could not stop crying.   Of course I was not aware of the danger of our predicament: the night curfew was approaching, if not already in effect, and a woman with a screaming child would attract not only sympathy but also the police and German soldiers.   However, at that moment a savior appeared, although he definitely didn't look like a savior: an old, bearded beggar, dressed in rags, shouldering a big burlap bag with all his worldly possessions.   He realized our danger, came to us, and standing over me he leaned down and said sternly that he'd to put me into his bag and carry me away unless I stopped crying and obeyed my mother. This was, in fact, a common threat used by Polish parents against disobeying young children, and coming directly from a grizzled old beggar with a burlap bag it had the intended effect on me: I immediately stopped crying, jumped up and hid behind my mother. I stayed quiet and very close to her until we reached our destination.

***

Leon and Family

Years after the war, when I became old enough to know and understand the war's major milestones in Poland – German invasion, September 1, 1939; Warsaw ghetto uprising, May 1943; Warsaw uprising, August 1944; Russian army pushes the Germans out of Poland, January 1945; war ends May 8, 1945 - I could overlay my childhood memories of events large and small on this timeline to determine roughly when these events happened. My mother told me that she smuggled me out of the ghetto in October 1942, before the mass round-ups and shipments of Jews to concentration camps and before the ghetto's uprising. This fits with the cold weather and snow that I remember on the night the old beggar scared me into silence and obedience with his burlap bag, which clearly happened outside the ghetto and thus within a few months of October 1942. After that event my mother moved me for my safety to different places several more times, so it must have been sometime in mid-to-late 1943 that she took me to live with Leon, his wife and their little daughter. I was 5 years old then, and I lived with them for about a year, past the August 1944 Warsaw uprising and into the winter of 1944-45.

I liked Leon. I don't remember anything specific about him other than his name, that he didn't have much hair on his head, and that I liked him. On the other hand, I clearly remember that I didn't like his wife, and that she often took the few things my mother would bring me on her visits, such as small toys or something good to eat, and give them to their little daughter who was a year younger than I. Perhaps that's why I don't remember their names, only Leon's. I envied the little girl, not only because she got the small gifts my mother brought for me but also because Leon and his wife took her outdoors for walks while I was never allowed to go outside - for my and their safety, but I didn't know that. However, I was allowed, in fact required, to leave the apartment each day, go down the staircase several floors to the basement where coal and potatoes were stored, and bring up heavy bucketfuls of coal for heating and cooking and potatoes for eating. It was hard work and I hated it.

One beautiful spring day is clearly etched in my memory – I now know it was spring because Leon's wife had bought a big batch of fresh rhubarb and made from it a very large bowl of compote. The window was open, and it was warm and sunny outside, and the sky was blue and beautiful. Leon's wife put the bowl of rhubarb by the window to cool, told me that they were all going out, and that I was not to touch the rhubarb while they were gone. I wanted so much to go with them, to be outside and play and run, but I knew they wouldn't take me. I stared at them through the window, watched them walk away down the street, started to cry, and then noticed the rhubarb. It was such a big bowl, I thought, that they would never notice if I had a spoonful, so I ran to the kitchen, got a spoon and tasted the rhubarb - it was warm and sweet and delicious. I looked at the rhubarb in the bowl, saw that there was no sign of the missing spoonful, and thus reassured I quickly took another one, then ran to the kitchen and replaced the spoon. I don't remember exactly what I did after first tasting the rhubarb, except that several times I repeated the sequence: checked the bowl, decided that another spoonful wouldn't be missed, got the spoon from the kitchen, ate a spoonful, and put the spoon back in the kitchen.

This back-and-forth continued until I suddenly started to feel sick to my stomach, and then realized that the sides of the bowl showed that it had been full and now was half empty. I could not believe that I had really eaten half the bowl one spoonful at a time, but the pain in my stomach told me that perhaps I did. Then Leon and family returned, and when his wife saw the half-empty rhubarb bowl she became furious, yelled at me, then told Leon to give me a good beating. And beat me he did, hard, over and over again. I was screaming, pleading with him to stop, until suddenly I felt not just the pain on my behind but also strong pain in my stomach plus nausea, and I started and continued vomiting rhubarb. I don't remember what happened next, but long afterwards I knew that I deserved the beating, and I still liked Leon, and I still liked rhubarb.

***

August 1944 - Warsaw Uprising

Summer was hard for me. I would stand at the window, see people walking and children playing in beautiful weather, and I was not allowed to go outdoors. It was even harder when Leon and family went out, leaving me alone in the apartment, standing at the window. Perhaps to keep me occupied, maybe even to prevent another fiasco like the rhubarb incident, Leon took notice of my curiosity and questions about newspapers that he read and started to teach me to read. Eventually, when they were about to leave me alone in the apartment, he would choose a newspaper article or two for me to read, then test me on the content when they returned and praise me when I did well. Only years later, with some maturity, did I truly appreciate how brilliant was his win-win scheme: it kept me occupied when I was alone in the apartment plus got praised afterwards, and they could leave with peace of mind. There was also another, totally unexpected bonus a year later after the war ended and I started school: since I could already read fairly well I was put directly into 2nd grade.

My first awareness of the impending catastrophe started one day while standing at the window, watching the summer from a distance: suddenly there was loud shouting on the street, people were running, and shots, many shots. Leon ran to the window, looked outside, and as bullets hit our building he grabbed me and ran back into the room, away from the window. For some reason, most likely ignorance, I did not feel frightened at that moment, and soon all was quiet. As Leon and his wife talked in very agitated voices, I remained unconcerned and oblivious of danger. Yet that night I had a dream that I still remember: standing on a low hill in near darkness I saw all around me a landscape of total destruction, with outlines of ruined buildings and burned, broken trees, with smoldering rubble, without life or movement anywhere. Then, suddenly, a huge flaming red devil flew across the dark sky, and I awoke in terror. The next night something happened that has never happened to me before or since: I had the very same dream, with the same ruined landscape and the same flaming devil flying across the sky and the same terror on waking. That afternoon we heard distant gunfire, and Leon's wife was packing suitcases and cardboard boxes. The next morning we all carried these downstairs and loaded them on a pedal-powered rickshaw (a 2-wheeled cart in front powered by a bicycle rear-end in back) that Leon had obtained somehow, and with him pedaling and his wife, daughter, and I sitting on the baggage, we left the city. The Warsaw uprising had started.

I remember nothing about the ride through the city, but once we reached the countryside there were fields of grain gleaming golden in the sun, farmhouses with thick thatched roofs, cows and goats in pastures, and occasionally people in the fields or on the road. It was quiet, except for Leon's pedaling and heavy breathing, and the rickshaw's creaking. Eventually we stopped to rest along the side of the road and I asked where we were going. "To my cousin's farm," Leon replied. I wandered away, along the ditch that ran beside the road, and then noticed a dark blue object, like a large potato, lying in the grass. I picked it up – it felt heavy and cold, like metal, and had a shiny ring on one end. I started to play with it, pulled on the ring, and it came out just as

Leon called to me that we were leaving. I tossed the object over my shoulder and it fell into the ditch, and I ran to the rickshaw. As I scampered onto it, there was a very loud bang from the ditch where I had just been. We all gasped, and Leon started pedaling furiously, much faster than before. It was only later, much later, that I understood that the dark blue object was a German hand grenade, and while Leon didn't know what I had done he did know that, with the uprising now in Warsaw, any Poles found by the Germans near weapons or explosives would be shot on the spot.

***

On the Farm

Leon's cousin had several sons, the oldest was 14 and the youngest was 6, same as I, and the boys all worked on the farm with the parents. The older boys worked alongside their father, doing man's work, while the younger ones did light work and clean-up. I was told to work alongside the youngest son and do what he did. During the next few months he and I spent much time together, doing chores, playing, even praying (more on that later), but I don't remember his name, so for the sake of this telling I'll call him Jan, Polish for John. One of the first tasks in which I helped Jan was clearing out the trash that had collected in their barn's attic, so the space could be used to store some of the upcoming harvest. I followed Jan up a steep wooden ladder to the attic – it was dark until he opened a shuttered window on the attic's end wall. There was much scattered trash all around, piles of old straw, some old potatoes, broken wood, etc, and we gathered most of it in old burlap bags and threw the bigger pieces down to the ground.

When we finished and were about to go down the ladder we heard above us birds chirping. We started searching and found, in the eaves of the barn's steeply pitched roof, a nest with several baby sparrows. Jan carried the nest with the baby birds down the ladder and we walked back to the farmhouse. Jan said he wanted to show the birds to his mother, but as we approached the house a couple of his older brothers noticed us and the nest Jan was carrying, ran to us and took the nest, saying that they'll show us a good game. They then called out for their dogs, and when the dogs came the older brother took a baby bird out of the nest, threw it down hard, and as it hit the ground the dogs lurched for it and the winning dog gulped it down. Then the other brother did the same with another bird, and they took turns throwing each of the baby birds to the frenzied dogs. I was stunned and horrified. Jan said nothing and went inside. I followed, shaken.

It was hot during the potato harvest, and Jan and I brought fresh drinking water to those who worked the fields. At the end of the harvest we helped with collecting the trash and debris and rocks that had accumulated on the fields during the season. Tree branches, dead bushes, pieces of wood and anything that burned were collected in one pile. Next to this pile a shallow hole was dug, filled with potatoes, then covered with dirt, and the wood and branches from the pile were put over it and lit. Nearby stood a barrel-like black metal tank and under it a fire was burning. This, I learned, was a vodka still.

Around sundown the burning trash was pushed off the place where the potatoes were buried, and the now-baked potatoes were dug out and given to those gathered around the fire. Cups of vodka, straight from the still and warm, were then given to everyone... except to Jan and me, at six years of age the youngest there. When Jan protested loudly at this discrimination I joined him, and the adults started laughing. Still laughing, they gave each of us a cup with just a little of the warm vodka, and as everyone downed theirs and bit into their baked potato, we did too. I had never tasted alcohol before so didn't know what to expect, but the warm liquid going down my throat felt good, and perhaps the bite of the baked potato smoothed out any harsh edges.

Seeing that Jan and I followed their example and downed our vodka, the men cheered, laughed, and poured another round for all adults. Encouraged by our success, we asked for more, but were ignored, so we asked again but in louder tones, perhaps a result of the vodka we had drunk. Jan's father stopped laughing, and with a very stern face said not only that vodka is for adults but if we asked one more time we'd have to go back to the house and go to sleep. I don't know if it was out of fear, anger, or the already-consumed vodka, but both Jan and I burst out crying. I don't remember what followed immediately, but only that there was singing around the fire and that we ate more potatoes.

After the potato harvest (late September 1944) not much memorable happened until Christmas, when I was introduced to prayer. Specifically, I was told to start saying prayers along with Jan each evening before we went to bed, and if I learned my prayers well I would also get the special dishes that were being prepared for Christmas. After that, Jan and I would kneel by our bed (which we shared), resting our elbows against it, and I would repeat Jan's words. However, since I didn't really understand the prayer, I asked Jan what it meant, and when he didn't know I asked him why he was saying it. "Because I was told to do it, just like you were," he replied. Fortunately for me, his prayer was so short that in a couple of days I could say it together with him, and the very next morning I proudly announced to his mother that I now could pray as well as Jan and therefore was eligible for those Christmas dishes. She tested me, and when I passed the test she patted my head approvingly and agreed that I could eat all the Christmas foods with Jan. My other memories of that Christmas are a jumble of scenes:

the hustle and bustle of food preparation in the kitchen, singing carols with others under light falling snow, kneeling beside Jan on the cold stone floor in a church and reciting prayers, and the Christmas table with beautiful dishes as I had never seen before.

***

Winter 1945 - The War Ends

I was no longer on the farm with Jan and his family. Sometime after Christmas or New Year my mother came to the farm and took me with her, and we were now together in another house in a village near Warsaw. There were many people in this house that, like us, were not part of the family, and that's probably why it reminded me of the house where I saw the soldier with the machine gun and where Lovichanka talked with my mother, long ago. Here too there was much activity and with new people coming and going, so it was different than on the farm, but now I was with my mother and I stayed close to her.

One night we were awakened by loud banging and shouting – my mother led me to the main room where everyone was already gathered. There were also three or four men whom I had not seen before, all in overcoats as if they had just come from the outdoors. One of the men had a pistol and was shouting orders. I watched as all adults stripped down to their underwear and put their clothing in the room's center. Then one of the men searched the clothing, another went around to each adult and demanded their jewelry and watches, while the one with the pistol continued to shout orders and wave the pistol. Eventually they left, and for a moment everyone was quiet, silent, and then the room erupted with crying and shouting, and the adults started recovering their clothing from the pile in the room's center.

A few nights later my mother woke me up again. She was teary but excited as she said to me "You are saved!", and then "Get dressed quickly." As she led me to the main room we passed a window, and in the darkness outside I saw soldiers in long winter coats and heavy hats and a huge dark shape: tank! As on the night of the robbers, everyone was gathered in the main room and there were several soldiers, but their uniforms were not the dark green color I saw in the ghetto uniform factory or on the German soldier with the machine gun that's still etched in my memory. Their uniforms were a lighter green, and they were not speaking German. "They are Russians," my mother told me. We stood there a few moments, and then the soldier around whom everyone had gathered noticed me, the only child in the room full of adults. He smiled, waved to us to come closer, and when I was directly in front of him he reached into his pocket and extended his hand toward me. Still smiling, he said something I didn't understand, and my mother told me to take it, that it's a cube of sugar for me. I put it into my mouth, tasted it, and it was wonderful! I felt the same joy as when I first saw the tricycle by my bed on my 3rd birthday.

Since the Germans retreated while the Russians or the new Polish government were not yet in full control, chaos and lawlessness prevailed in the countryside, such as the robbery in our house a few nights earlier. Nevertheless, the main danger to us had been the Germans and now they were gone, so my mother felt it was safe enough for me to be outside, to play in the snow, and to go with her on a very long walk to obtain food. Everything was covered with fresh white snow, so my mother borrowed a small sled and pulled me on it part of the way to a farmhouse which was our destination. At the farmhouse she got a big bag of potatoes, a small bag of flour and another of sugar, and a small package of butter, a rare treat. When these were loaded and tied onto the sled my mother gave the seller a small gold cross that she had been wearing. I was surprised to see it and that the robbers didn't get it, so she told me that she had hidden it very well, and I was very impressed at how smart she was.

With the sled loaded with bags of food and my mom pulling it through the snow along the road's edge, I walked at her side and chatted with her. Since food, especially tasty food, had been a luxury ever since I could remember, I became really excited when she started telling me what wonderful dish she would make for us when we got home. Focused more on the vision of the upcoming feast than the road, I apparently drifted to the side and, all of a sudden, was head over heels in the snow that filled the ditch. I gasped for air as my mouth filled with the soft snow, and my mother pulled me out and dusted off the snow that totally covered me. When we got home, she made the feast I had been waiting for: plain flour-and-water dumplings boiled in water and topped with a bit of butter, which was a luxury, and for dessert a handful of dry flour browned slowly in a skillet and then mixed with sugar. I slept full and happy that night.

A few weeks later we returned to Warsaw by train, arriving at a station somewhere on the city's periphery, and then we walked to the city center. It was a clear, bright day, with small patches of snow here and there, and where we started our walk the streets were quiet and undisturbed: a few people, a few horse-drawn carts, and occasionally a military vehicle driving by. Then, as we neared the city center, the scene changed radically, becoming the desolate, devastated landscape I saw in the dream that repeated itself two nights in a row in August, immediately before the Warsaw uprising started. However, what was a dream then was real now: ruins of buildings everywhere, streets filled with rubble, craters large and small everywhere, and between the rubble and the craters were narrow, winding paths that people had worn with their footsteps.

As we turned onto a less devastated street, a man's body was lying ahead of us, a bit to the right of where I was walking. My mother quickly pushed me over to her left side and we passed the body. I felt that her intent was to protect me, but I was nevertheless puzzled, as I had seen bodies lying on streets during our ride out of Warsaw as the uprising started and I felt no fear or danger from them. I was considering asking her why she did that when she announced that we would walk to the other side of the Visla River, to the Praga suburb, because it was not destroyed and there was an apartment where we would stay. Soon we were walking on a pontoon bridge across the Visla to Praga. Years later, after we left Poland, I learned that the Praga section of Warsaw was not destroyed during the August uprising because it was already occupied by Russian troops. However, they offered no support to the pro-Western Polish underground which staged the uprising, thus allowing the Germans to exterminate the Polish fighters and thereby facilitating the Russians' subsequent occupation and domination of Poland. This bit of history was certainly known to most adults but it was never discussed publicly or taught in schools, so children didn't know it.

***

Spring 1945 - Up from the Rubble

From the ruins and devastation and the sometimes-chaos-sometimes-silence that was Warsaw when my mother and I returned to the city in late winter, spring saw life emerging slowly from the rubble like the proverbial green shoots. As streets were cleared of the rubble, one by one, and the craters from bombs and cannon shells were filled, pedestrians appeared and so did traffic, mostly military trucks and cars, plus horse-drawn carts, as ubiquitous in the city as they were in the country and on farms. On the main streets even the sidewalks were being cleared, and on those appeared not only pedestrians but also sellers of basic items: food, used clothing, hand tools, pots and pans, matches, whatever the seller could hold while standing or spread on the sidewalk while sitting.

One of the foods sold by many of these vendors was canned pork, packed in military olive-green cans with black printing in Russian describing its contents. This widely-sold item was known by its Russian name "Svinaya Tushonka", and it was common knowledge that it was supplied by "our friends, the Russians" to save Poland from hunger. Only years later, shortly before we left Poland, did someone point out to me that near the cans' bottom edge were very small Latin (not Russian) letters "Made in USA". Contrary to the propaganda-induced common knowledge, this was part of the goods that the U.S. shipped to Russia under America's Lend-Lease aid program, and Russia, in turn, re-shipped it to Poland and to the other countries it occupied, claiming that it was Russia's gift to them.

One day my mother and I were walking along a main street where many sidewalk vendors were selling various goods. Suddenly my mother stopped and asked me whether I recognized a blond woman sitting on the sidewalk a few steps ahead of us. Yes, I answered, it's Lovichanka. My mother gripped my hand tightly, walked up to Lovichanka and in a very firm voice said to her: "Long ago you wanted to call the police on my son. We're ready to go to the police with you now." Lovichanka's face turned white, then bright red, and she started protesting that it was not her, that it's all a mistake, that she would never do that to a child. My mother glared at her in silence, then told her that we would walk a little further, and then we'd come back and go with her to the police. We did walk a block or two further, and when we returned a few minutes later Lovichanka was gone. It was then that my mother explained to me what happened that day two years ago, and why she took me away from that house in the evening and how the beggar who threatened me with his burlap bag was a godsend.

As Warsaw began coming to life my mother got a job as a manager in the new book publishing enterprise "Ksiozhka" ("Book" in Polish), which was owned by the Polish Communist government along with all means of production and the media. Since part of her responsibility was establishing Ksiozhka bookstores in the Warsaw region and other cities, and since there was still a fair amount of banditry (post-war chaos) and political unrest (resistance to the Communist take-over), she was assigned a driver/bodyguard, a pre-war 3-wheeled car (with very limited top speed), and a pistol (which, luckily, she never had to fire). I was proud of her when she told me about all that.

My mother Pauline and I, 1945-46

She also said that to celebrate the new job she would buy me something that fascinated me every time we had walked "downtown", and I knew immediately that it was a marzipan. A candy and confectionary store had opened in the same undamaged space that, according to my mother, it had occupied before the war, and its display window boasted a beautiful platter of fruit-shaped marzipan candies: red strawberries, yellow apricots and dark plums, and miniature apples and pears and peaches. Every time we passed the store I was mesmerized by their colorful display and fascinated by the idea that all these different fruits were somehow the same sweet substance which, of course, I had never tasted. I still remember that each of the small pieces cost 100 zlotys, which I knew was a large sum but had no idea what it really meant vis-à-vis anything else since I never had any money and thus never bought anything.

I was very excited as we walked to buy the marzipan, and when we arrived at the store I wanted to stand at the window for a moment, taking in the beautiful sight of the display but with the knowledge that one of these would be mine. When my mother asked me which one I wanted I was actually surprised – I was so excited and focused on the moment that I had not even thought about making a choice. I snapped out of my reverie and, after some thought, decided on a bright red strawberry. When my mother paid the 100 zlotys and I was given the marzipan strawberry, I carried it out of the shop very carefully, like a priceless jewel, and once outside I took small, measured bites, to make it last as long as possible. The taste was one I had never experienced before, and I was in a momentary heaven. Marzipan has remained my favorite confectionary to this day, and on my 50th birthday in Los Angeles my mother gave me 50 marzipan strawberries.

***

Summer 1945 - Returning Prisoners, Falling Stars

Several times during those early months after the war my mother and I went to the railroad station on the news of trains arriving from Russia carrying Polish prisoners from the Eastern front. (When Germany attacked Poland in September 1939 from the West, the USSR attacked it from the East, as had been agreed by Hitler and Stalin and formalized in the Molotov-Ribbentrop pact.) My father, an attorney and reserve officer before the war, was called to active duty in the war's first days and sent to the Eastern front, and my mother hoped that he had been taken prisoner and would be returning from Russia on one of these trains.

My mother was understandably filled with hope and anticipation as we waited for these trains to arrive at the station, but for me it was a strange, unsettling mix of expectation and concern. On the one hand, I wanted a father in my life and quietly envied those children who had one, such as Leon's daughter and Jan on the farm. On the other hand, I had no memories of my own father as I was only one year old when he left for the front, so the train for which we were waiting might bring a total stranger who would enter our life, and I could only hope that I would like him. Together with a lot of other people we would stand at the station's entrance and watch as the gaunt and bedraggled men filed out, slowly and wearily. Sometimes there were joyous shouts as the waiting and hopeful spotted one of their own, followed by much embracing and tears of happiness. Mostly, however, the arriving men shuffled by ungreeted, perhaps because they were not from Warsaw and had to travel further to find their families, or perhaps because there were no survivors in their family to greet them. My mother was always quiet when we left the station after finding no one. We would walk home in silence.

My father Julian Elbaum, 1938

One evening that August my mother and I were riding in a car on the pontoon bridge across the Visla River. I presume it was some business function because it was her company car (now upgraded from the old rickety 3-wheeler to an old rickety 4-wheeler) and her driver/bodyguard. It was a clear night, and the whole starry sky was visible across the open expanse of the water. However, unlike most nights, the sky was full of falling stars – it really looked like it was raining stars, or like the whole sky was falling. Then I recalled an old Polish superstition that each falling star signifies someone's death, and I wondered whether these hundreds and thousands of falling stars represented those who had died in the war, perhaps including my father. Since then I've happened to be a few times in the mountains or desert on a clear night in August during the Perseid star shower, and I am always struck by the difference in my circumstances and conditions then and now, and how lucky I am for this difference.

On my 7th birthday that August my mother told me that we would go to two stores which she and my father patronized before the war and which had recently re-opened. The first was a shoe store named Rachek where my father bought his high quality shoes and where she now wanted to buy me a good pair to replace my old torn ones that were too small and hurt my feet. Rachek did have some children's shoes to choose from, and my mother and I chose a very nice pair of light brown dress shoes which, I now realize, were about as practical for an active 7-year-old as a tuxedo on a camping trip. Though I was too young to understand it, my mother probably wanted to buy me something representing the quality of life she knew before the war, and Rachek shoes fulfilled that role for her. I obviously also wanted them. There was just one problem with our choice: the smallest pair in stock was 2 sizes too big for me. However, with both of us wanting to buy them and the salesperson wanting to sell them, a 2-part solution (justification, to be more accurate) was concocted: first, the shoes should *really* be one size larger than my feet so I would not outgrow them too quickly; next, the salesperson would fill the toes of the 2-sizes-larger shoes with cotton to make them only one size larger. With all 3 of us eager for a solution, I proudly walked out of the store in my beautiful new shoes, the first real present I received since the tricycle on my 3rd birthday.

From the Rachek shoe store we walked to our next destination, perhaps 15 minutes or half hour away. After a while I noticed that my new shoes were not totally comfortable, but it hardly mattered because I was so thrilled to have them, and to see my mother's beaming face when she said several times how beautiful they were and how similar to a pair my father had bought there before the war. As we walked, my mother told me that we were going to an ice cream and dessert parlor which she and my father and their friends had all patronized. My thoughts galloped: I've never been in a café or a restaurant or eaten ice cream, and I'm doing it all on my birthday in my new shoes! We sat at a small outdoor table in front of the café and my mother ordered for me one of their specials: three ice cream scoops, vanilla, chocolate, and raspberry, in a silver metal dish on a short pedestal, topped with whipped cream and waffle cookies stuck into it. As I sat there on that beautiful August day, eating my first ice cream whose wonderful flavors and creamy texture I could barely believe, wearing my new shoes, and being with my mother, I was filled with a feeling that only years later, as an adult, I would describe as an overwhelming "all is fine with the world."

A few days (or perhaps weeks) later I experienced an equally strong but painful feeling. I was playing in our courtyard with another boy from our building when he referred to another boy as a "dirty Jew." While I considered myself a Catholic because the several families with whom I had lived brought me up as one, even at the young age of seven I apparently had a strongly liberal bent and countered my playmate's slur by declaring that there were good Jews and bad Jews, just as there were good Poles (meaning Catholics) and bad Poles. He disagreed with my view, and sufficiently so that it escalated to a noisy and eventually physical altercation. My mother happened to witness some of it, questioned me about it later, and decided that the moment was right to tell me that she and I were Jewish, as had been the rest of our family and that's why they didn't survive the war. I was stunned! I didn't know what to say, what to think.... and then I started crying! Only much later was I able to admit to myself that, in my belief in fairness, I was willing to defend Jews but I didn't want to be one.

***

Life Becoming Normal

By autumn 1945, only eight months after Poland's liberation from the Germans, life was apparently starting to become normal in Warsaw. I, of course, recognized this only in retrospect, as at that time I had not yet known "normal" life and thus had no basis to even know what that meant. For example, normalcy meant that in September children go to school, and since I was no longer in hiding from the Germans and had just turned seven, I would be starting 1st grade. Indeed I did so, and on the first day of school I proudly told my teacher that during the summer I had read a children's science book entitled "300,000 kilometers/second" (the speed of light), and therefore I already knew everything about science that the school would teach. Although the teacher was probably quite amused by my assessment, she didn't let on and thus didn't deflate my over-confidence; rather, she handed me a book and asked me to read from it. Apparently I read well enough so the next day I was in 2nd grade.

Another aspect of normalcy, at least for Communist Poland, was that not only the Post Office but also the censors were working sufficiently well so mail and care packages from America were now being delivered. My mother had a second or third cousin, Pearl, living in New York, and somehow they connected (through the American Jewish Joint Distribution Committee, I believe), and Pearl's letters were soon followed by care packages filled with puzzling but delicious foods. Perhaps the most puzzling at first were marshmallows, because I knew of no plant or tree that produced such "fruit." Another puzzle was canned peaches, whose shape and texture reminded me of the peaches I ate on the farm but whose taste was totally different, obviously some unknown-to-me American fruit. Still another puzzle and a disappointment were M&Ms: while I liked their chocolate insides, I expected each color covering to have its own flavor and hoped the red ones would be either strawberry or raspberry, my favorites, yet the only flavor was chocolate, nothing else. I wondered why clever Americans didn't think of having different flavors for the different colors.

On the other hand, everyone agreed that American cars were very, very impressive: big 4-door Chevrolet, Ford and Plymouth sedans with shiny chrome could be seen near the American embassy on Avenue of Stalin, which I would pass going to and from school. Especially after school, when there was no hurry, I and other kids would stand near the embassy to get a glimpse of these cars and perhaps see some other, more unusual brand, such as an occasional DeSoto or Packard. American embassy cars easily outshone all other cars on Warsaw streets, be these pre-war German Opels, French Citroens, Czech Tatras, or the military Jeeps used by Russian officers (supplied by the American Land-Lease aid program). For me and other boys, the only cars in Warsaw that came even close to the American sedans were the couple of Russian ZIS limos from the Russian embassy, and even though these didn't look as impressive as American cars, we had already swallowed enough propaganda to say between ourselves (and believe) that ZIS cars were sturdier and more reliable.

A similar but even more extreme case of propaganda swaying young minds (and probably many mature ones also) was the prevalent opinion of Warsaw's trolleys. The first year or two after the war Warsaw had only Russian-made trolleys that sported peeling paint over cracking plywood bodies. Then Warsaw got some trolleys from France: modern-looking, metal bodies, good paint, smooth-riding. Since it was difficult to deny their much-better appearance and ride, the generally-accepted story was that while the French trolleys had better bodies, the Russian ones had better, stronger motors. As kids, we didn't look for proof, but accepted the circulating "common knowledge" as the truth. Not all adults, of course, outgrow such thinking.

Perhaps the only dissonance that we as children sensed between Russia and America was exhibited in our reaction to the free films at the American embassy. By the embassy's entrance there was a wall-mounted, glass-faced case in which the embassy posted public announcements (in Polish) and photos to interest the passers-by. Periodically the embassy showed free films, often about the war, and the photos of battles and weapons shown in the glass case always fascinated young school-boys. However, on several occasions I and some school friends stood in front of the embassy intending to see one of the war films, yet none of us dared to be the first to go inside, and eventually after much you-first-no-you-first we would sheepishly walk away and go home, never quite knowing why we couldn't do it.

***

America or Palestine

It was many months later, sometime in 1946, that I met my very first American. Actually, he was one of my mother's pre-war friends who managed to escape from Poland and immigrate to America, and now he was a Captain in the American Army on assignment in Warsaw. The first time he came to our apartment in his crisp uniform he brought several foods that I had never seen before, perhaps from the American embassy or some store which was not open to ordinary Poles, and with these my mother made a great dinner for the three of us. One of these foods that particularly impressed me was watermelon: I could not imagine how something so green on the outside (and thus, from my experience, not yet ripe) could be so red and so sweet on the inside. In the following months he came to our apartment several times, always bringing some special food which we ate for dinner together. During his visits my mother and he talked about life before the war and life now, as she did with other old friends, but he would also tell her about life in America, and a few times when I listened to their conversation and asked him a question he always answered it clearly and completely, and was very nice to me in general.

Ironically, one of his food gifts resulted in my doing (or rather not doing) something that to this day I still regret. That gift was a single banana, the first banana I had actually seen in life rather than in books about Africa. I was about to taste my very first banana when there was a knock on our door: it was Szymon, my friend, classmate and neighbor, with whom I had a fight that morning but we more-or-less made up on our way home. When he saw the banana his eyes grew large, as mine surely did when the American gave it to me. He asked me about it and I told him that it was a gift from my mother's American friend, and that I was about to eat it. I took the first bite, savored the banana's unfamiliar and wonderful taste (a taste which even now can remind me of that long-ago moment), and then noticed that Szymon's eyes were riveted on me and the banana. My mind raced through conflicting thoughts: the banana is wonderful; Szymon wants a bite; I have only this one banana; he's a good friend; we had a fight this morning; we made up coming home; we didn't *fully* make up; we made up enough; yes, but I don't want to give up even one bite; who knows if I'll ever get another banana. That is where it ended, and to this day I wish that I had given Szhymon a bite of banana.

Szymon (on right) and I, 1946

My mother had another pre-war friend who, like the American, got out of Poland when the war started and now returned as a French citizen working for a humanitarian aid organization. He would also visit us when in Warsaw, have dinner with us (although without bringing food gifts like the American), and he would talk to my mother about Jewish life in Palestine. He was not as friendly towards me as the American and seemed to barely tolerate my questions. Eventually my mother told me that he was trying to convince her to emigrate and go to Palestine, while the American was offering help in immigrating to America.

***

1947 - To France and Back

I don't know why I never asked my mother exactly how or why it happened, but in early 1947 I was on a train with several dozen other Polish-Jewish orphans or half-orphans bound for France, and from there we would sail a few months later for Palestine (Israel was not established until 1948). So, two years after the war ended I was once again embarking on another long separation from my mother. I don't quite understand why I didn't ask her at that time why she was doing it, or in the years or decades since. Perhaps the reason is that the continuous separation I experienced during the war acclimated me to it, made me accept it as a normal life, and thus I no longer questioned it. Perhaps, but I'm still not sure. In retrospect, I realize that two years after the war's end there was still much anti-Semitism in Poland, including some pogroms and killings, and the chance of another war and Holocaust did not seem impossible. Since immigration to America was a long and difficult process, perhaps some event pushed my mother into deciding on Palestine as a chance for our safety, so she sent me now and would join me later, a separation like the ones I experienced during the war. Whatever the exact reason, I was on a train to France with several dozen other children.

In France our group was housed in a big country house, a beautiful old chateau near Paris. Most of the children in my group were about my age, 8 to 12 years old, with a few in their teens. Much of each day was spent in classes preparing us for life in Palestine: learning basic Hebrew, local customs and folk songs. We certainly didn't just study, but also had fun in organized games, soccer, various social activities such as camp fire gatherings with singing and dancing, and time to play on our own. It was probably a couple of months after we arrived in France that we were told the good news: in two weeks we would be leaving for Palestine.

My passport photo 1947

A few days later, after dinner, a few of us were chasing each other when someone stepped out in front of me and I tripped, twisted, fell, and my leg hurt terribly. One of the staff was called, examined me, and said that I might have a broken leg so tomorrow they would take me to a hospital. Because the war left many people in Poland without a leg or an arm, I assumed that if a limb is broken it must be amputated. Thus as I lay on the floor, thinking about spending the rest of my life on one leg, one of the boys with whom I had just been running tried to comfort me by saying that tomorrow I'll be playing soccer with him again. The thought raced through my mind: how can I ever play soccer on one leg! Then I started crying. The next day I was taken to a hospital where the French doctor X-rayed my leg, confirmed that it was broken, and said that he'd be putting a heavy cast on it. When the doctor's words were translated for me into Polish, I was totally confused: "Why do all that if they'll be cutting off my leg?" I asked, trying not to cry.

A week later, after the other children left for Palestine, the chateau was almost empty except for the remaining staff and me in a heavy leg cast. Several weeks later I was taken to the Paris airport, where I boarded a Polish military transport (it was a DC-3) with a long row of bench seats along each side, most of them empty. Once we were flying it became very cold inside the airplane; then one of the pilots came out of the cockpit and showed us how to use long black rubber hoses through which warm air was flowing.

Of the few other passengers on board, one was a striking looking woman with black eyes and black hair pulled back on her head. When we landed in Warsaw one of the pilots made sure that she was the first one at the exit door. When the door opened, I could see a large crowd of people with many flags, Polish, Russian, plus a third flag I didn't recognize, and a band playing marching music. Who are they welcoming, I wondered, certainly not me. Later I learned that the striking woman was a famous Spanish Communist known as La Pasionaria for her fiery oratory during the Spanish civil war. I realized that it must have been a real feat for my mother to arrange my return to Warsaw on a government plane together with this dignitary, and I was very impressed. However, just as I never asked her why she decided to send me to France and Palestine in the first place, I never asked her how she arranged my return.

***

How My Mother Survived

It was probably after my return from France that I was old enough (age 9) to realize that I was relatively sheltered from the Nazis through the war by being raised by Polish Catholic families, and how difficult survival must have been for my mother "out in the open". I don't remember asking her specific questions, but I started paying attention to the anecdotes and stories she occasionally told me and from these forming a mental image of how she survived the war years. My mother came from a family of well-educated, economically-comfortable Polish-Jewish intelligentsia. Both she and her older brother were college-educated, spoke French and English, and she finished law school shortly before I was born. My father was a practicing attorney and his family owned a brewery in Kazhimiezh, a historic town near Warsaw.

All this was gone within two years of the German invasion in September 1939: my father was called into the army immediately after the invasion and never returned; some months later the Germans came for him to our apartment and, since he was gone, took my grandfather who also never returned; my uncles and their wives were taken and vanished under similar circumstances. After my mother arranged for my grandmother a place in the supposed safety of a "bunker" (a long-term hiding place which was subsequently betrayed by the man who delivered its food stockpile), only my mother and I remained.

My mother and her brother Mjetek as children, 1920

As her various family members disappeared and she smuggled me and herself out of the Warsaw ghetto, she did retain two marketable assets from her pre-war life: her education and some valuable jewelry. After escaping the ghetto she placed me with the first of a series of Polish Catholic families, and to pay these families for my care and for their risk in hiding me from the Germans she sold her jewelry, one piece at a time, to get the needed cash. She also dyed her hair blond, bought "Aryan papers", real or forged ID documents of (probably) deceased Polish Catholics, and worked a series of jobs. She first worked as a French governess for a wealthy Polish family who wanted their daughter to speak French, then as an English governess with some home maintenance and cooking (where she felt sorry for her employers because she had never cooked before, yet they were nice enough not to complain about her cooking too often), and when her French or English were an unnecessary luxury she worked as a cook and housekeeper. To avoid being traced by the authorities through the faked ID documents she, as others in similar situations, bought a new set every so often, and it was the name on the most recent set of documents that she would have me memorize the next time she moved me to a new family.

My mother Pauline, 1946

Ironically, it was my mother's most prosaic job, as a cook and housekeeper, which proved to be the most dangerous. Her employers were well-to-do Poles who wanted good fresh food which required her to make almost daily trips to food stores, and every trip to a public place meant another chance of encounter with German soldiers, document inspection, questioning, and discovery. One encounter in particular stood out in my mother's mind because she told me about it several times. She was food shopping in a neighborhood store when she noticed a uniformed Gestapo officer on the sidewalk outside the store, looking at her through the store window. The Gestapo were feared much more than ordinary German soldiers because of their leading role in the "Final Solution" of Jewish extermination and their brutality. When the Gestapo officer entered the store and continued to stare at her, my mother realized that she was truly in great danger, but also knew that if she tried to leave the store he would definitely stop her, demand her documents, and that could lead to deportation and death. Though shaking with fear inside, she forced herself to continue perusing the vegetables, carefully choosing the best ones and trying hard to seem nonchalant and unconcerned. After several minutes, when she had selected several vegetables and didn't think that she could hold any more in her hands, the Gestapo officer suddenly turned around and left the store. For a moment my mother didn't know what to do next, perhaps to drop everything and run, but instead she quickly bought the vegetables she had gathered and walked home at a measured but not overly-hurried pace. Survival: luck, strength, and wits.

***

1949 – To France Again

In early 1949 my mother told me that in a few months we would be moving to Paris together. As a manager in the government book publishing company, she was being sent for a couple of years to establish and manage a chain of Polish book stores in France for the many Poles who immigrated there mostly before the war. It was quite unusual that I was allowed to go with my mother to France – whenever the Communist government sent someone to a Western country they always kept some family members at home as security against defection. However, no one else in our family survived the war and could care for me if I remained in Poland, so an exception was made in our case.

In preparation for our move my mother started buying certain things; since Polish money could not be legally taken out of Poland (nor did it have any value abroad), and since we would presumably return to Poland after her foreign assignment, the only items that we could take with us were personal and normal household items. Thus whatever money she'd saved during the 4 years of working at Ksiozhka she converted into things of real value that could pass for our household items, even though a bit luxurious, which we'd be allowed to take with us: a 12-place set of sterling silver tableware (but whose bright finish she ordered dulled to make it look used), several antique silver serving dishes and decorative pieces that reminded her of those that had been in her parents' home, two Persian carpets at least 100 years old, beautiful hand-embroidered tablecloths, and the like. While she liked these items for their beauty, their fine quality, and the memories they evoked in her (and 20+

years later she used them or displayed them in her Los Angeles home), she bought them with a war-time mentality focused mainly on their marketability, the possibility of converting them into cash if an unexpected need ever made it necessary to sell them.

My focus, on the other hand, was on my stamp collection; started a year or so earlier and collected with a passion, it was a wonderful tool for learning geography (issuing countries), fauna and flora (subjects represented), and it was visually striking because it was full of very picturesque and odd-shaped stamps (triangular, diamond, etc) of small, poor countries such as Mongolia and Tuva that issued these beautiful stamps not primarily for use as postage but as a source of revenue from sales to inexperienced stamp collectors, such as I. Thus my collection had little monetary value, unlike those of serious philatelists, but this was not evident to the Customs officials to whom my mother submitted the list of our belongings the day before we were to leave for France. When she returned home from the Customs office and told me that they would not allow us to take the stamp collection abroad, I was heartbroken. I tried to explain to my mother why it was not valuable to anyone but me, but it was difficult to talk while crying. Apparently my mother understood enough, in spite of my crying, so she grabbed the stamp collection and managed to get back to the Customs office before they closed, and when she returned home she told a very happy 10-year-old that the Customs official agreed that my collection was not worth very much.

Only two memories remain from our train ride from Warsaw to Paris; both seem trivial, yet both have persisted for six decades. Shortly after the train left Warsaw I took from my backpack the very last marshmallow that I'd been saving from the last care package we received from my mom's cousin Pearl in New York. I savored it one small bite at a time and, watching the fast-moving landscape, I wondered whether we could buy more marshmallows in Paris or whether we'd have to ask Pearl to send some from New York, or whether I would ever have another marshmallow in my life. On a more serious note, after the train crossed into France (and beyond Communist Poland and East Germany) my mother took out our tube of toothpaste, pointed to the rolled-up bottom end, and very quietly told me that she had opened that end and hid some U.S. dollars inside as emergency money, so if something happened to her I should know about the dollars but tell no one. (Citizens of Communist countries were not allowed to own U.S. dollars or other freely-convertible currencies.)

***

Paris 1949

We arrived in Paris in late spring, and the next few months passed smoothly and uneventfully. We lived in a small apartment near Metro La Motte Picquet, and I quickly learned the whole Metro system, so even before I could speak French I could find my way around Paris and explore it using the Metro while my mother was at work. On a typical day of exploring Paris I would choose a Metro station, ride there, walk around the surrounding neighborhood and "take in" any special sites that particularly interested me, then ride the Metro to another station and repeat this process, eventually returning home. My favorite outing was to the Jardin des Tuileries and its large circular pool where children sailed toy boats – I would watch them with a mixture of envy and acceptance, and a feeling that someday I too would have my own "petite bateau" and sail it there.

My mother and I in Paris, 1949

This routine changed when Mark Whiteman came to Paris mid-summer. Mark was my mother's distant cousin from Poland who managed to make his way to the U.S. in 1941, and somehow my mother and he made contact with each other when we were in Paris. (I say "somehow" because I don't know how, and here again I never asked my mother, and I don't know why I didn't.) After a month or so they were married and my mother resigned from Ksiozhka and thus became a Polish defector. She then applied for an American visa under a "preference quota," as she was now the wife of an American citizen, and Mark returned to the U.S. and awaited her arrival. (Under the preference quota a visa would usually be issued in a month or two rather than years for most wartime refugees seeking the safety of America.) Since I had no legal relationship to Mark, I did not qualify for the preference quota; this would have to wait until my mom was in the U.S. and he could apply to adopt me, which would make me also eligible for the preference quota with fast visa issuance.

By the time my mom's visa was issued in September she had found a French-Polish couple with whom I would stay the couple of months till my visa would probably be issued, and then I would fly to America. A short time after getting her visa my mother left for America and I was once again alone and living with strangers. However, I was now old enough to understand and appreciate the difference between the current situation, when I could look forward to being reunited with my mother in America, vs. those during the war, when I understood very little except that occasionally my mother would visit me and then go away again. After my mom's departure I continued to spend my days riding the Paris Metro, visiting various neighborhoods, watching Parisian children sail their little sailboats in the Jardin des Tuileries pool, and upon returning to the apartment each day asking the couple with whom I was staying whether they'd received any news of my visa. This pattern lasted for almost three months, but finally one day in late November I asked my daily question and this time the answer was "yes!"

It still surprises me that my sole memory of this couple and their apartment is a plastic tablecloth imprinted with a faux embroidery pattern that covered their dining table. It was the first plastic tablecloth I had ever seen, and I was terribly impressed by its practicality: its "embroidery" pattern was similar to those on the fancy handmade tablecloths that my mother bought immediately before we left Warsaw for Paris, yet any spill could be easily wiped off the plastic without a trace. Practicality beat aesthetics hands down! I felt that I was truly seeing the future, and I was impressed.

***

Air France to New York

On December 1, 1949, I boarded an Air France Lockheed Constellation airliner for a long, long flight to New York. As an 11-year-old flying alone Paris-to-New York, I got special care and attention from the flight attendants, probably enhanced by being quite small for my age and speaking broken French. I had flown once before, in 1947 from Paris to Warsaw on a DC-3 military transport with hard benches for seats and hot air blowing through rubber hoses to keep any passengers warm against the freezing temperature at altitude, so the amenities and comfort of a trans-Atlantic airliner were more than I could have imagined. For the first hour or so I simply sat in my seat, looking around at everything in view and touching anything that I could reach. Then I decided to go exploring, so I asked a flight attendant about a toilet, and she took my hand and led me to it, explained how to use the flush and the faucets, and how to lock the door. I then proceeded to look at and try everything in the toilet rather than really using the toilet as intended.

My passport photo 1949

A short time later the attendants served a big, sumptuous meal, and because it was really big and sumptuous it ended in a traumatic experience for me. Beautifully arranged on the tray were more courses than I had ever seen: a bite-size appetizer, a salad, a jelly-covered something with a design on top, a hot main course, a cheese course, and a beautiful dessert. It all went well until I got to the jelly-covered something, which turned out to be cold crab. For some reason I have always hated seafood (even now I tell waiters that if it lives in water I do not eat it) and the first bite of the crab stopped me cold: I hated it, no ifs or buts, but wartime experiences conditioned me to eat everything on my plate. I took a deep breath and forced the crab down one small bite at a time until it was all gone. It was painful but it was done, I thought, and moved on to the main course, and then the cheese. However, though I love cheese I was already very full and struggled to finish the cheese course.

Now it was time for dessert, and I love desserts as much as I hate seafood – in fact, an all-dessert meal has always been my ideal. It was at this moment that I realized how absolutely full I was, actually over-full and starting to be nauseous, and that I could not possibly eat the beautiful dessert that was in front of me on my tray, the dessert that I'd been viewing with anticipation while forcing down the crab. The sudden realization that I could not eat the dessert, that I would leave it untouched while I had forced down the horrible crab, was just too much for me, and I started crying, quietly at first and then not so quietly. Almost immediately an attendant came over and in a very motherly voice asked me what was wrong. Even while crying, I realized how silly it would sound if I told her the truth, that I was crying because I could not eat the dessert, and that made me embarrassed as well as feeling sorry about the dessert, so I cried even harder. Soon another attendant came and they both tried to soothe this crying child who would not tell them why he was crying. Eventually I stopped crying, or rather the crying simply stopped, and the attendants walked away puzzled.

***

New York, December 1, 1949

The Air France flight arrived in the afternoon, and my mother met me at the airport together with her cousin Pearl, whose care packages to us in Poland contained such mysterious-to-me products as marshmallows, canned peaches, and the colorful but disappointingly one-flavor M&Ms. Pearl was a short, plump woman, somewhat older than my mom, and her genuine warmth was so evident that even though I didn't understand a word of English (the only language she spoke) I instantly liked her. At the baggage claim we were met by a man in a black suit and cap (Pearl's chauffeur, my mom told me), who took my small suitcase and led us to a Cadillac limousine. (I did expect all Americans to have cars, but I didn't expect that they also had chauffeurs.) We drove into the city, and Pearl suggested (as translated by my mom) that I may want some refreshments or ice cream since I'd been flying for so long. The thought of my uneaten dessert on the airplane flashed across my mind and was replaced immediately with the thought that American ice cream must be as good as all other things American, and now I would get to taste it. Pearl took us to a restaurant by the name of Rumplemeyers – it specialized in desserts and children and was on Central Park South (it's been closed for over 30 years now). When she described the various ice cream specialties I learned that a dish called "sundae" included not only several flavors of ice cream but also a banana and chocolate syrup and a red cherry, so obviously that was the dish to have as my first meal in America. It would even make up for the dessert I couldn't eat on the airplane.

While we were waiting to be served, Pearl told us that in

America boys my age (11) wore long pants rather than the shorts that I was wearing (like European boys), and that we should buy pants for me tomorrow. It was after this conversation that I asked about a bathroom and Pearl (via my mom) gave me the directions, including the critical signage on the doors: "Ladies" and "Gentlemen." I followed the directions, found the two doors, but the signage was different: one had a big M and the other a big W, and I did not know what these meant, or what happened to "Ladies" and "Gentlemen." I decided to wait until someone else came to use the toilet, and based on which one they used I would know which one I should use. However, when no one came after several minutes and I realized that the wonderful-sounding "sundae" dish I had ordered was probably waiting for me and starting to melt, I made a choice of doors (on what basis I don't remember), went inside and into one of the stalls. It was only a few seconds later when the door to the bathroom opened and someone else walked in and entered the stall next to mine. I looked down beneath the partition and saw a pair of woman's legs and heels! A sudden feeling of panic, but then relief because I was not wearing the long pants we planned to buy for me tomorrow, and the realization that my bare legs could just as well belong to a girl. I waited till the woman left the bathroom and then flew out of there at full speed and into the other bathroom. Only when leaving this bathroom a few minutes later did I look back at the door I had just exited: it had a big letter M, while the other door had a big W. I would definitely not forget this!

For a cultured adult the highlight of Pearl's apartment might have been its walls, which were absolutely covered with dozens and dozens of small paintings of Napoleon – any free wall space was clearly fair game for her collecting passion for Napoleon miniatures, and there was painfully little of it left for any new acquisitions. For me, however, the highlight was her television, the first one I had ever seen. Covering its small circa-1949 screen was a big, thick magnifying glass, like a giant monocle, which for me only added to its imposing mystique. The only program I remember watching was Howdy Doody, which seemed a bit childish to me. However, since I had elevated everything American to a mental pedestal, I told myself that the dialogue, which I didn't understand, had to be more substantial than the childish visuals. Howdy Doody aside, it was the television itself that was so impressive.

My only disappointment in things American was Coca Cola. While in Paris I heard much about Coca Cola as the most popular drink in America and tasting like nothing else, so in my mind it had to be something extraordinary, perhaps on par with the big, impressive American cars and New York skyscrapers. In my mind, Coca Cola was the taste of America. Obviously those were very high expectations, and since in such cases reality is usually disappointing, Coca Cola was no exception.

***

Cove City, North Carolina

From New York my mom and I travelled to Mark's home in Cove City, NC: 1500 population, the white half living on one side of the state highway and the black half on the other side. Most people were farmers, with tobacco their main crop, a few were loggers in the pine forest of that area, and a dozen or so worked on a small sawmill that Mark owned. There was a general store on each side of the highway, on weekends a movie theater in a tent with wooden benches showed cowboy movies, but for more excitement one had to drive 17 miles on the state highway in one direction to Kinston or in the other direction to New Bern, where there were regular stores, movie theaters and cafes. After living in Warsaw and Paris, tiny Cove City seemed very provincial even to me at age 11, and much more so to my mother.

Since I did not speak English, one of the first topics my mother, Mark, and I discussed together was the best and fastest way for me to learn the language. The result was a 3-prong program, and at the time I felt it was a joint decision but now I realize that my mother and Mark had probably arranged it all beforehand. First, in our house we would speak English as much as possible and only if I didn't understand something would I ask in Polish. Next, I would start going to the 6th grade (I was in the 5th grade when we left Warsaw that spring) as soon as the local school opened after the New Year, where I would be in an English-only environment. Finally, at the end of each school day I would get a private lesson in English from Mrs. Heath, the 6th grade teacher who didn't speak Polish. Another early topic of discussion and a "major decision" for me was my American name. My Polish name was Jerzy, which translates into George (all Polish names are of saints, and Saint Jerzy is Saint George), so George was listed on my adoption papers and that was my American name - period. However, George sounded too formal to me at age 11, too much of King George of England, so Mark suggested that Jerry sounded and looked like Jerzy. I liked it, so I decided to use Jerry as my nickname, and to this day it's been Jerry in my personal life and George in business and the like. (The adoption also changed the last of my several Polish names, Kochanowski, to Mark's last name, Whiteman, but after he was killed in a car accident a few years later I changed it to Elbaum, my father's name with which I was born.)

Mrs. Heath, who taught me English, was a tall, gentle woman of around 30, with curly brown hair, glasses, and a heavy Southern accent, though I did not realize it was an accent. To this day I can still see her face. At the end of each school day she tutored me for about an hour by showing me flashcards with a drawing of some object, such as a horse, the English word "Horse" for that object, and she would then pronounce that word slowly and have me repeat it after her several times. There were two flashcards and words that, for different reasons, I had great difficulty understanding. The first was "Barn," with the flashcard showing a typical American barn with a metal roof and a cylindrical silo, but to me it looked like an industrial building, since Polish barns at that time were always large wooden sheds with thatched straw roofs, no silos and no metal anywhere. The other word was "Water," and it was clear to me that the drawing represented the surface of water with ripples on it, so there wasn't any cultural misunderstanding.

However, since Polish is phonetic I read the word as "wahter", while the word Mrs. Heath pronounced sounded to me like "waaarah." I resolved my confusion by deciding that in English there must be two words for "water", one being "water" and the other "waaarah." This solution worked for me until about a year later when we moved to Oregon and I noticed that no one there used the second word, "waaarah", and I asked my mom for an explanation.

Mrs. Heath had a son, Dalton, who was also in the 6th grade and quickly became my best friend in Cove City. It was Dalton who did his best explaining to me the basics of baseball so I could join the game in my first week of school, and then getting me off home plate after 3 strikes when I kept insisting on getting two more tries by raising my hand and showing 5 fingers - I had somehow gotten into my head that 5 strikes was the limit, not 3. Dalton had a crush on Shirley but was too shy to make it known, so he coached me to ask her "Do you like Dalton?". When she answered me "I like you both" I was very puzzled because I knew of no one in our class named Both, so for Dalton's sake I then asked her "Who is Both?"

School lunches during my first couple of months of attending 6th grade were for me occasions for discovery, sometimes amazement, and sometimes disappointment. One of my first discoveries, though clarification is probably a more appropriate word, is that the delicious but unidentifiable canned fruit that Pearl occasionally included in the care packages she sent to us in Warsaw and that tasted like no fresh fruit I knew was, in fact, peaches. I say "clarification" because all it took was my asking Mrs. Heath about it and her showing me a colored picture of a peach in a book. Eggplant, on the other hand, was a more difficult issue, and "amazement" is truly an appropriate word here. After tasting fried eggplant for the first time in a school lunch, I liked it but could not identify it. As with the peach, I asked Mrs. Heath and she showed me a colored picture, but unlike the peach I could not identify it because eggplant was unknown in Poland at that time. However, with its beautiful purple color, smooth shape and shiny skin, it was unlike any vegetable I had ever seen and I was absolutely amazed that a vegetable so beautiful exists at all. Since it clearly did exist, though, it seemed appropriate to me that it existed in America, the land where anything was possible. Lunch-time disappointments, on the other hand, occurred every time fish (especially smelly fish) or some other seafood was served, as I hated and still hate seafood. At those times I would use the two ingredients always available in the school's cafeteria, sliced white bread and mustard, and I would make for myself a "mustard sandwich". While bread with mustard was not my favorite lunch, I did remember that only 5 years earlier I would have considered it a good meal.

An unexpectedly memorable experience was my first bus ride in America. We were in Raleigh, North Carolina's capital, and my mom and Mark left me with his local friend while they conducted some business. At the appointed time the friend put me on a city bus whose route ended in a place where my mom and Mark would meet me. Even though I hardly spoke English, this seemed quite simple to me considering some of my previous travels alone. Indeed it would have been simple and not at all memorable had I not taken a seat near the back of the bus. After driving a short distance the bus driver apparently noticed in the rear view mirror where I was sitting, stopped the bus, walked back to where I sat and started talking to me, presumably telling me to move forward to the whites-only seats.   While I understood some of the words, I understood nothing of the concept, so I answered him with "I don't speak English."   At first he seemed confused (perhaps I was the first foreigner he'd met), then exasperated, till finally he leaned over and (as I was small for my 11 years) picked me straight up, carried me forward and put me down in one of the front seats.   I gasped for air, said nothing, and was very, very glad when I finally got off that bus and met my mom.

Tourist in Smoky Mountains, 1950

***

Summer 1950 at Camp Carlyle

As summer approached, my mother and Mark told me that in America, as in Europe, children sometimes went to a summer camp, and that it would be both good for me and fun to spend a month at such a camp with American children in an English-only environment. Thus a few weeks after the end of school in Cove City we drove to Camp Carlyle located in a forested area near Hendersonville, NC. We arrived there in the evening, and when all the formalities, arrangements, and introductions were completed, Mark and my mom left and the counselor to whose group I was assigned asked me if I'd had dinner. I had not, so the counselor explained to me (with some difficulty, since my English was still quite limited) that it was long past the camp's dinner time so the kitchen was locked for the night, and the only food stored outside the kitchen was potato chips. Would I like some, perhaps with a Coke? I did know Coke, and I knew potatoes, but what were potato "chips"? I tried one and I was instantly hooked, so that evening I gorged myself on potato chips and Coke, my very first "on my own" dinner in America.

Camp Carlyle was, in many other ways, my real "on my own" introduction to America, its people, its customs, and its natural bounty. The camp was on a small lake where we swam, surrounded by woods where we walked, ran, and played team games, and it had horses, stables and a riding ring where we learned riding and caring for the horses. I loved it. One of the all-American things to which I was soon introduced was Cracker Jack, the boxes of candy each with a surprise gift inside, and I would buy it (for 5 cents a box, I think) at the canteen after most dinners, charging it to my account - another first in learning all-American customs. Another custom, or rather attitude which was much different than in Europe at that time, was the American openness about money or wealth, as when another camper who was also about 12 years old asked me point blank if my father was wealthy. I was totally taken aback, and only after a moment could I answer (honestly) that I had absolutely no idea. A less important though almost as puzzling experience for me was learning at the camp's award ceremony at the end of our session that I was the camp's shuffleboard champion, since I did not understand the counselor's explanation of the game's rules and thus had no idea where the puck should land and where it shouldn't. Presumably that's a perfect example of beginner's luck.

My most memorable experience at Camp Carlyle was, unquestionably, my first "dake." This obviously requires an explanation. One evening each week we would clamber on the back of the camp's open-bed truck, drive into town, see a movie in the town's one movie theater, and at a pre-arranged time meet the truck and return to camp. After a couple of weeks I noticed that some of the boys and girls were paired up: they got onto the truck together and stayed together through the evening. When I asked one of the boys about it, he said they were "going out on a dake" - at least I thought he said "dake", though of course it was "date" – and that the boy pays for the movie tickets. I thought that "when in Rome do as the Romans do" and for the next week's outing I asked Connie from Charlotte, NC to "go with me on a dake." (I remember that she was pretty and that I could understand and speak with her easier than with most other kids.) She accepted, so we rode on the truck together, saw a movie (for which I paid "as the Romans do"), and after the movie Connie asked me if I wanted to get a hamburger. I was still so far from being Americanized that I had to ask "What's a hamburger?" She very nicely told me that she would show me and took me to the local café, at which point I realized that I did not have enough money for two hamburgers - the boy who explained "dakes" to me spoke about paying for movies but nothing about hamburgers. When I told Connie that I had enough money for only one hamburger, she very graciously said that we could split one. Afterwards we got back on the truck with the other kids to drive back to camp, and were chatting with relative ease.

I liked Connie and felt very comfortable with her. It was at that point that Eddie, one of the older boys who was at least 14, asked me if Connie was my "dake." I was puzzled momentarily - while I knew that one "goes out on a dake", I did not know that the other person was "your dake." Guessing from Eddie's question that it was so, I answered that she was. "So why aren't you holding her hand?" Eddie asked. I was taken aback, embarrassed: I had enjoyed our "dake" and talking with Connie, but I felt no need to hold her hand, yet per Eddie's question I was apparently supposed to do it. So, should I do it now, or was it too late? Did I make a faux pas or was holding hands not really important? Confused and embarrassed, I did not take Connie's hand and was no longer comfortable or enjoying being there with her. The sad upshot of that "dake" was that I did not go on another one for more than 3 years, till my third year in high school. ***

7th Grade in Cove City

A month in the English-only environment at Camp Carlyle made me almost fluent in English, which means I was almost fluent when I was doing the speaking and could choose the words I already knew. However, because my vocabulary was still quite limited it also meant that I didn't understand many words that were being said to me, so I often had to ask the meaning of a word or a phrase. Still, I felt comfortable with English when 7th grade started in September.

My first surprise was the school's fall schedule: classes ended at noon so all children could return home to help their parents with the tobacco harvest! My understanding of a school schedule was still the European 6 days a week, and here it was not just 5 days but in the fall it was 5 half-days! Thus even though I left Poland half-way through the 5th grade and a year later entered half-way through the 6th grade in Cove City, I still had no problems with any subjects other than my lack of English. Now that I was "almost fluent", I found the more universal subjects such as math or world history or geography in the 7th grade to be very easy because I studied the same material in the 5th grade in Warsaw. I remember thinking that Cove City grade school could surely not be typical of American schools, otherwise American education could not have developed the technology and industry that was the world's most advanced and powerful. (Though I was right about that, the subsequent decades have shifted the advantage not to America's favor, and that continues to sadden me.)

Because 7th grade was so easy academically and I was bored most of the time in school, my mother suggested that I consider skipping 8th grade when we moved to Oregon over the summer, which we planned to do because timber, the raw material for Mark's sawmill, was getting harder and harder to obtain in North Carolina. (We did move, in fact, selling the current sawmill and buying another one in Oregon together with enough timberland to assure our own supply of raw material.) Our main concern about my skipping 8th grade was that I might get too far ahead of myself socially, but decided to go ahead with it. As it happened, a good example of my social underdevelopment occurred still in Cove City's 7th grade - in retrospect, it was a hilarious but private highlight of my school year, not something to tell one's parents.

The school had launched a contest between the classes to collect green stamps or gold stamps for the school. The 7th grade won the contest, and our reward was to be released from one class and allowed to go outside and play. We all went outside and my small group of several boys and one girl found ourselves on the ball field near a shed. Though I did not realize it, as we were walking one or two of the boys were trying to talk the girl, Maggie, into "playing house" with us, and as we neared the shed she agreed. It had been not long beforehand when I learned that "playing house" meant having sex, which some 7th and even 6th graders in this small farming community were already doing, and apparently that included Maggie. However, I was 12 years old and had no sexual feelings as yet, so the whole subject was more of a local curiosity for me than something that I felt personally. All this changed suddenly when Maggie, having agreed to "play house" with us one at a time, chose me to start the game. I stood there, dumbfounded, as I really had no idea of what to do if I went to the shed with Maggie, and my hesitation and confusion were obvious. Finally one of the boys asked why was I not going with Maggie, and I felt the same embarrassment that I felt at Camp Carlyle when Eddie asked why I was not holding Connie's hand. I searched my brain for a good answer, and in total ignorance and defensiveness I blurted: "We don't do that in the big cities." My hesitancy, or perhaps my answer, seemed to change the mood, because the next boy Maggie chose also said "no", and we eventually drifted back to the school. However, to this day I wonder how long after that outing did the others learn that actually we do "do it" in the big cities, and what was their reaction to this news.

***

Forest Grove, Oregon 1951-1955

We did move to Forest Grove, Oregon in the summer of 1951, and I had an interview with the principal of the high school. The last question he asked me (and the only one I still remember) was on which continent was Egypt located. I visualized a map of the Near East, answered "Africa", and he said "You can start 9th grade next month." I had just turned 13, and while I was definitely underdeveloped socially and had more in common with the school's nerds than with its athletes, I no longer felt like a foreigner but rather like an American.

The only time I came to doubt the comfortable feeling of being an American was while seeing a speech therapist in Portland a year or so later. My mother took me to the therapist because my stuttering had increased. While I don't remember when I first started stuttering, my mom said that it was when one of the families with whom I lived supposedly told me that she had been killed. The stuttering was never bad or debilitating because whenever I got stuck on a word I could usually find an alternate one to use, but in early high school I decided to "force it out" by auditioning for a school play where I had to use the scripted words, no fudging. My "force" method failed me in the audition when I couldn't say the starting word "you" in the phrase "You look just like the dying gladiator, without the beard." I obviously didn't get the part, and my mother took me to a speech therapist for professional help. During the first session the therapist had me read a poem (John Masefield's "I must go down to the sea again"), recorded it, and played it back to me. This was the first time I heard my own recorded voice, and I was horrified: first, I didn't know that we hear our own voice differently from all sounds coming to our ears "from the outside" because we also hear it "from the inside" via our head's cavities and bone structure; and second, the voice I heard coming from the tape recorder had a strong Polish accent whereas I thought that I no longer had one. I was shocked, I was mortified, I wanted to stop speaking so not to be embarrassed by that horrible accent! Perhaps if I only whispered I would solve both the stuttering and the accent problems! These and other declarations came and went, dissolving in the daily flow of reality, but slowly I managed to handle both issues and even got a part a year late in the senior play. However, that sudden realization which hit me while in my early teens, when we want so much to fit in and embarrass so easily, was very painful.

Forest Grove High School freshman, 1951

***

Boston 1955: "Never again"

Within a month or two of entering Massachusetts Institute of Technology I reported to the school's infirmary for some administrative reason. The issue was handled by a nurse whom I remember as a friendly, middle-aged woman, and as we chatted she asked where I was from. "Oregon, but originally from Poland," I replied. She asked when did I come to the US and I replied that it was in 1949, only 4 years after the war ended. She said that she was from Vermont but came to a nursing college in Boston and stayed ever since. Then she said: "Those horrible things that supposedly happened in the war, like those newsreels showing concentration camps in Poland, those things didn't *really* happen, did they?" I was stunned. How could this college-educated woman raised in New England with full exposure to the wartime news be in doubt that the Holocaust really happened? How could she ask me to validate her doubts? It was unbelievable. I stood there in shocked silence. Then it struck me: she was asking me because she didn't want to believe that it happened. I was appalled and I snapped back: "Yes, it did happen. I was there, I lived through it!" Her face showed little reaction or emotion, and I realized that she didn't believe me. It wasn't the answer she wanted, so she ignored it – she didn't, or couldn't, let it register.

I left her office feeling frustrated and helpless, and that feeling returned to me in subsequent years whenever I encountered the hopeful slogan "Never again." Given this nurse and countless others like her, I felt that "Never again" regarding the Holocaust specifically or genocide in general was but a wishful fantasy. We believe what we want, and we deny what we don't want, so what hope, what chance is there for "Never again"? None with those like that nurse. Yet there might be a chance with most others who are more open-minded, uninformed, or unconvinced. Therefore, those of us who did experience the Holocaust must somehow convey, to even a small degree, our experiences, our feelings, our loss and our hope to a new generation, and inspire them to convey it onward. The first responsibility is ours..... and that's why I wrote my story.

***